The Ghosts of London: A Collection of Ghost Stories from the British Capital

By Sean McLachlan and Charles River Editors

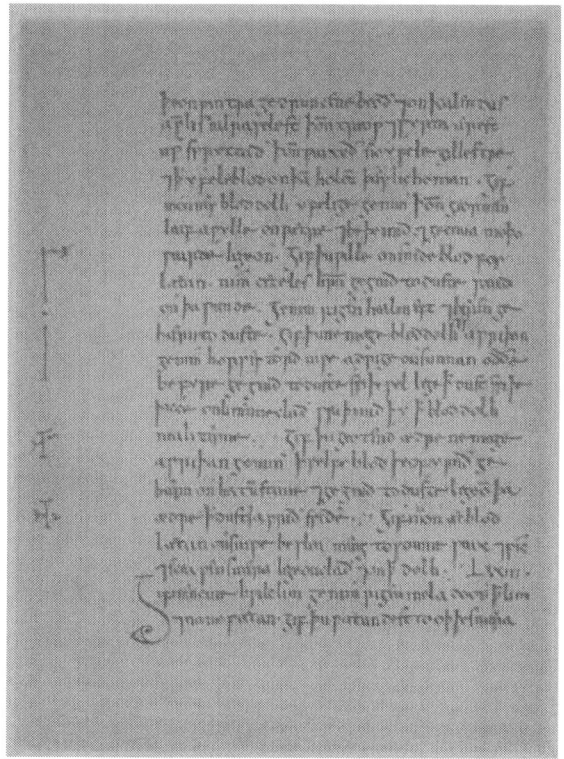

A page from *Bald's Leechbook*

About Charles River Editors

Charles River Editors is a boutique digital publishing company, specializing in bringing history back to life with educational and engaging books on a wide range of topics. Keep up to date with our new and free offerings with this 5 second sign up on our weekly mailing list, and visit Our Kindle Author Page to see other recently published Kindle titles.

We make these books for you and always want to know our readers' opinions, so we encourage you to leave reviews and look forward to publishing new and exciting titles each week.

About the Author

Sean McLachlan spent many years working as an archaeologist in Europe, the Middle East, and the United States. Now a full-time writer, he's the author of many history books and novels, including _A Fine Likeness_, a Civil War novel with a touch of the paranormal. Feel free to visit him on his Amazon page and blog.

Introduction

An Anglo-Saxon belt buckle depicting the god Woden (Odin)

The Ghosts of London

England is an ancient land steeped in history and tradition, filled with prehistoric ruins, majestic castles, and a countryside sculpted from millennia of human habitation.. Its rolling countryside is dotted with prehistoric burial mounds and stone circles. Brooding castles hold tales of bloodshed and honor. Medieval churches have elaborate stained glass windows and gruesome carvings, reflecting a mixture of hope and darkness. Every hamlet and village has tales that go back centuries, and folk festivals with roots in pagan times.

Thus, it is not surprising that many believe England is a land filled with ghosts. For centuries, people have told tales of ghosts stalking its historic buildings, strange creatures lurking in its primeval forests, and unexplained paths linking its ancient sites. And naturally, as one of the world's most historic capitals, every step in London takes visitors through hundreds of years of history laden with stories of political intrigue, war, romance, and the inspiration of artistic and scientific geniuses. From the most magnificent avenues and monuments to the humbler minor streets and private homes, it seems every brick and cobblestone has a story to tell.

The English are enchanted with the spirits of the dead. They are woven into the legends of historic buildings and take a prominent place in English literature, from Shakespeare and Dickens to modern writers such as Peter Ackroyd. So many buildings, streets, and even Tube stations have resident ghosts. Here is a collection of such tales, from among the hundreds of local legends and modern sightings that make England one of the most haunted countries in the world.

The Ghosts of London: A Collection of Ghost Stories from the British Capital offers a sampling of the many strange ghost stories and unexplained phenomena that make London such an intriguing place. Along with pictures of important people, places, and events, you will learn about the ghosts of London like never before.

The Ghosts of London: A Collection of Ghost Stories from the British Capital
About Charles River Editors
About the Author
Introduction
    The Cock Lane Ghost
    Famous Landmarks
    The Most Haunted House in London
    Haunted Churches and Cemeteries
    Haunted Pubs
    Underground Ghosts
    Room 333: The Haunted Hotel Room
    Just Plain Weird
    Online Resources
    Further Reading
Free Books by Charles River Editors
Discounted Books by Charles River Editors

The Cock Lane Ghost

A 19th century depiction of Cock Lane

Ghosts have been reported in London since the Middle Ages. Doubtless, there were earlier sightings since been lost to history. The first really sensationally famous ghost—the infamous and controversial Cock Lane Ghost—appeared in the mid 18th century. This haunting was made famous through the writings of Dr. Samuel Johnson, a leading writer and wit of the day whose enduring contribution to English letters was the compilation of the first extensive dictionary of the English language. His biographer, James Boswell, wrote a detailed account of his life and travels and had much to say about the hauntings at Cock Lane.

Johnson

In 1759, church clerk Richard Parsons lived in a modest home on Cock Lane, near St. Paul's Cathedral. A heavy drinker, he faced money troubles and took lodgers in to support himself, his wife, and his two daughters. That year, his new lodgers were William and Fanny Kent who had arrived from out of town; Fanny was pregnant. Richard was happy to take on the new tenants, especially when William agreed to lend him some money.

The two families got along well, and William soon confided a scandalous secret to his landlord: he and Fanny had been living in sin. William had, in fact, been married to Fanny's sister who had died in childbirth. The baby soon also died. Richard and Fanny had grown close during this tough time and decided to live as husband and wife, although such a union was illegal at the time. They had moved to London to get away from Fanny's disapproving family and live in peace.

For a time, nothing strange happened at Number 20 Cock Lane until William went out of town on business. Fanny felt nervous sleeping alone and asked Richard's eldest daughter, Elizabeth, who was 11, to share her bed. Sharing a bed was common practice at the time, so no one thought it unusual—the unusual part came soon enough.

One night, Fanny and Elizabeth heard a strange knocking on the wall. At first, they thought it was the cobbler next door, but it happened every night thereafter, even on Sundays when the cobbler didn't work. Richard tore out the wainscoting to look for the source of the sound but could not find any.

An illustration of the room where the haunting took place

Shortly thereafter, William and Fanny moved to a house they had been fixing up in Clerkenwell. Richard decided that since he was losing lodgers, the best way to make ends meet was to avoid repaying the money he owed William. This made William take the church clerk to court, at which point Richard spilled the beans that he and his pregnant "wife" had been living in sin.

As the fight grew ever more acrimonious, Fanny grew ill and was diagnosed with smallpox. The strange rappings at the Cock Lane house continued, too, and Richard Parsons became convinced it was the spirit of William Kent's dead wife, angry at Fanny for having seduced her husband. An indistinct, ghostly figure with a bright glow appeared on the stairs and was witnessed by both Richard and a neighbor.

Fanny died on February 2, 1760, and William soon found himself in a dispute with her family over her will. Fanny had left almost all of her considerable savings to William, and her siblings took him to court, saying that he should get nothing.

Meanwhile, back at Cock Lane, the rapping continued. Richard Parsons felt his house haunted by two ghosts: William's original wife and Fanny, as well. Desperate to be rid of the noisy spirits, he called in the help of Reverend John Moore, rector of St. Bartholomew the Great church in West Smithfield.

Moore held séances in the house and got in contact with the entities, using the simple technique of getting the spirit to rap once for yes and twice for no. The Reverend discovered the hauntings to center around young Elizabeth. This is typical of poltergeists, unseen spirits that manifest themselves by making noises or moving objects. Their activities tend to occur around girls approaching or passing through puberty. Moore discovered the noises were most frequent in Elizabeth's room after she had gone to bed. The rapping came from the walls, floor, and ceiling. Other noises, such as scratching and the fluttering of wings, occurred there, too.

Through a series of séances, the spirit revealed itself to be Fanny. She claimed that William had poisoned her and she demanded justice.

By then, the hauntings had attracted the attention of the press, which is where William Kent first learned that the ghost of his dead wife had supposedly accused him from beyond the grave. William went to speak with the reverend himself and attended a séance, where the ghost bluntly accused him of murder. Incensed, William stormed out.

The press coverage had turned the Cock Lane Ghost, now known as "Scratching Fanny," into the sensation of the season, and people crowded into the house to hear the knocks for themselves. Various tests were done to rule out fakery. Elizabeth's hands and feet were held down, and the rapping continued. The girl's physical and mental state had begun to deteriorate; she suffered from fits and claimed the ghost had visited her swathed in a shroud and without hands.

Since the famous hauntings included the accusation of a crime, the public demanded an investigation. The Lord Mayor asked Stephen Aldrich, vicar of St. John's, Clerkenwell, to lead it. Aldrich brought in several leading figures, including Samuel Johnson, to attend another séance. This time, it would be at Aldrich's house, with Elizabeth in attendance. After the séance, the committee was to visit Fanny's coffin in the vault of St. John's, where the ghost was to knock on the coffin to prove its existence.

The séance was held on the night of February 1, 1762. Boswell wrote about it in his *Life of Samuel Johnson*: "On the night of the 1st of February many gentlemen eminent for their rank and character were, by the invitation of the Reverend Mr. Aldrich of Clerkenwell, assembled at his house for the examination of the noises supposed to be made by a departed spirit, for the detection of some enormous crime. About ten at night the gentlemen met in the chamber in which the girl, supposed to be disturbed by a spirit, had, with proper caution, been put to bed by several ladies. They sat rather more than an hour, and hearing nothing, went down stairs, when they interrogated the father of the girl, who denied, in the strongest terms, any knowledge or belief of fraud. The supposed spirit had before publickly [sic] promised, by an affirmative knock, that it would attend one of the gentlemen into the vault under the Church of St. John, Clerkenwell, where the body is deposited, and give a token of her presence there, by a knock upon her coffin; it was therefore determined to make this trial of the existence or veracity of the supposed spirit. While they were enquiring and deliberating, they were summoned into the girl's chamber by some ladies who were near her bed, and who had heard knocks and scratches. When the gentlemen entered, the girl declared that she felt the spirit like a mouse upon her back, and was required to hold her hands out of bed. From that time, though the spirit was very solemnly required to manifest its existence by appearance, by impression on the hand or body of any present, by scratches, knocks, or any other agency, no evidence of any preter-natural power was exhibited. The spirit was then very seriously advertised that the person to whom the promise was made of striking the coffin, was then about to visit the vault, and that the performance of the promise was then claimed. The company at one o'clock went into the church, and the gentleman to whom the promise was made, went with another into the vault. The spirit was solemnly required to perform its promise, but nothing more than silence ensued: the person supposed to be accused by the spirit, then went down with several others, but no effect was perceived. Upon their return they examined the girl, but could draw no confession from her. Between two and three she desired and was permitted to go home with her father. It is, therefore, the opinion of the whole assembly, that the child has some art of making or counterfeiting a particular noise, and that there is no agency of any higher cause."

Thus ended England's first official ghost investigation. Soon afterward, Elizabeth was found fetching a piece of wood before another séance, and the assumption was that she had used this to make the noises.

It all seemed to be a matter of fraud, and Richard Parsons and his wife were brought to trial. Richard was found guilty of fraud and sentenced to two years in prison plus three sessions in the pillory. The pillory, also called the stocks, was a device set up in a public place to hold a prisoner's head and arms immobile so the prisoner could be abused by the crowd. It was a combination of punishment and mass entertainment, with eager citizens throwing rotten produce and animal droppings at the hapless convict. Mrs. Parsons was given a year in jail for her part, while Reverend Moore got off with only a fine, albeit a hefty one.

After Richard Parsons got out of jail, he tried to redeem his reputation. He pointed out that he had never made any money from the ghost's notoriety, and he had never been in trouble with the law before. He had some supporters who said they had heard noises so far away from Elizabeth that she couldn't have possibly faked them. How, they asked, could she have made noises come from the other side of the room or the ceiling? And what about the ghostly apparition the neighbor had seen?

Richard Parsons never cleared his name, but a strange footnote to the story surfaced years later. In 1850, an illustrator named J. W. Archer, visited Fanny's coffin in the church vault to make some sketches for a book. He got the caretaker to open the coffin and found Fanny's body remarkably preserved after having been dead for 90 years. Even the cartilage of her nose was intact, although cartilage is one of the first parts of the body to decay. Archer examined Fanny's skin and could see no signs of the smallpox of which she supposedly died.

A noted effect of arsenic poisoning is that it preserves the corpse.

Famous Landmarks

London's many historical buildings are filled with spirits from the past.

One of London's biggest attractions is Westminster Abbey, the outstanding site of coronations since the Middle Ages. Possibly built on an old temple to Apollo, the site was made Christian in 610 AD by King Sæberht of the East Saxons when he converted to the new faith. In 960, a Benedictine abbey was built on the spot. King Henry III began construction of the present building 1245. Later kings and queens have added to and expanded the building. With its two soaring western towers—designed by Sir Christopher Wren and completed in 1745—it stands as one of the great landmarks of the London skyline. The interior of the abbey is beautiful, with its lofty Gothic ceiling and giant stained glass windows. There are also the smaller details, such as the tombs of many royals and other leading figures.

Gordon Joly's picture of Westminster Abbey

It is at one of these tombs that a ghost supposedly lingers.

For some, it is the most moving grave among the hundreds there, because it does not have a name on it. A simple, black flagstone is inscribed with the epitaph:

"Beneath this stone rests the body

Of a British warrior

Unknown by name or rank

Brought from France to lie among

The most illustrious of the land

And buried here on Armistice Day 11 Nov. 1920"

This man was one of thousands who had either died in World War I and were buried in unmarked graves or whose bodies were never found. The Unknown Soldier came to symbolize the sacrifices of an entire generation. Queen Elizabeth, the Queen Mother, laid her wedding bouquet on the tomb. Before she died in 2002, she said that she wanted her wreath not to be placed on her tomb, but to be placed on that of the Unknown Soldier. Many people, both great and humble, feel an equal attachment to the tomb almost a century after the end of the war.

It is not surprising, then, that a spirit lingers there. Visitors have said they have spotted a man in a World War I uniform appearing out of thin air next to the tomb in quiet times in the abbey, bowing his head in quiet respect before fading away. Perhaps the man isn't so much a ghost as he is the spirit of a nation.

A less somber ghost said to walk within those hallowed walls in the early evening is that of a medieval monk named Father Benedictus. He seems quite jovial and will chat with visitors, which is unusual for a ghost. He's been seen there since around 1900.

London is one of the greatest theater cities of the world, counting many of its theaters among its historical landmarks. As such, they tend to have a lot of ghosts.

One of the city's oldest and most renowned theaters is the Theatre Royal Drury Lane, where there has been a playhouse on the spot since 1660. When the first theater was built, it was one of only two sanctioned theaters in the city, as the stage was seen as a source of bad social influence and thus highly suspect. The present building dates to 1812. While it's not as impressive as its sister theater, the Theatre Royal Haymarket, it has a stunning interior and hosts a string of popular shows.

Elisa Rolle's picture of the site today

The theater isn't just home to a lot of dramatic history, but a few remaining star performers call it home. Perhaps the most famous of these is Joseph Grimaldi (1778-1837), a pioneering entertainer who invented the whiteface clown makeup so familiar today. Grimaldi might have died more than a century ago, but he's still clowning around at the Theatre Royal. He is occasionally seen as a faint figure on stage, but he is usually felt more than seen. If he doesn't like an actor, he's even liable to kick him in the rear!

Grimaldi

Another clown that haunts the stage is Dan Leno (1860-1904), who played a variety of comedic roles to packed houses. His most popular roles were in the cross-dressing shows at the Theatre Royal, where he would dress up in outlandish clothing and play various female roles, including that of Mother Goose.

Leno

Like many comedians, Leno also had a darker side. An alcoholic, he began to deteriorate in later years and developed incontinence. To cover up his occasional accidents on stage, he would wear a heavy, lavender perfume. His mental state also went downhill, and he spent some time in a lunatic asylum. While there, he complained to a nurse that the clock in his room told the wrong time. When assured that it was correct, he quipped, "Well if it's right, then what's it doing here?"

Leno always liked to have the last laugh, and he's still having one today. Sometimes, actors on stage at his old haunt (pun intended) smell his lavender perfume. Yes, after all these years, Leno is still messing his trousers, but at least he's not kicking people in theirs!

A more serious ghost is the mysterious "Man in Grey." Unlike the other two ghosts, no one knows who he is. He sometimes appears as a grey, indistinct figure who looks like he's wearing a tricorner hat, which would make him a contemporary of Joseph Grimaldi. Once, in 2012, a few employees sitting in the upper circle during a performance and talking amongst themselves were startled when one of their seats shook, and the man in grey appeared, whispering, "Shhh."

Some theater workers believe the Man in Grey is the ghost of someone who might have been murdered in the building. When the theater was renovated in the 1840s, human bones were discovered behind an upper circle wall. A knife was found, stuck in the ribs, the logical assumption being that the person was murdered and the body walled up to hide the evidence. Who this man was and if he truly is the Man in Grey remains a mystery.

Despite all these hauntings, the Theatre Royal remains a good place to see a play. The show must go on, after all.

The Dominion Theatre over on Tottenham Court Road opened as a cinema in 1929 and hosted the London premiere of *City Lights* by Charlie Chaplin in 1931 when the great comedian, a Londoner born and bred, was in attendance. In more recent years, it has found success as a theater popular with the tourist crowd.

The site in 2017

What the tourists don't usually know is that the Dominion Theatre was built on the site of a bizarre tragedy. The Horse Shoe Brewery, one of many local breweries in London at the time, used to stand on the very spot. The brewery housed several large vats, the largest of which was for porter and contained more than half a million liters of beer. On October 17, 1814, at around 6 p.m., the vat burst, and the force of the explosion under so much weight shot fragments of wood, parts of the barrel's metal hoops, and a jet of beer at the neighboring vats. These broke, too, and a tidal wave of beer burst through the brick wall of the brewery. Some 1.25 million liters of beer poured into the adjoining slums. Two houses collapsed under the onslaught, and several more were badly damaged.

Londoners haven't changed much—the local reaction was to swarm into the area with any bucket, bottle, or cup handy and down the free beer. The taste might have been a bit off, though, thanks to all the rubble mixed in, as well as the bodies of people found floating in the smelling mess. Nine people died - eight from drowning or injuries, and another by alcohol poisoning from drinking too much of the beer.

The area was an impoverished one, and the grieving families didn't have the money to pay for funerals, so they took to exhibiting the bodies at a price for curious visitors. At that time, sideshows were all the rage—what better show than the corpse of someone who died drowning in beer? This caused a second tragedy, when the poorly made floor of one hovel—no doubt weakened by the flood—gave way, sending the entire crowd into the basement, which was still half-full of beer. Sadly, none of these idiots died, but it did prompt the police to step in and ban the exhibition.

One of those killed was 14-year-old Eleanor Cooper, a barmaid at the Tavistock Arms. The pub was close to the brewery and partially wrecked in the tidal wave. Eleanor's body was found crushed beneath the rubble.

Now, it is said poor little Eleanor haunts the Dominion Theatre. She appears as a frail, pale figure with a menacing look on her face. She's given more than one theater-goer a bad fright, although she has never actually attacked anyone. She was even photographed in 2012.

One of London's most unique attractions is the Charterhouse, one of the few townhouses from the Tudor era to have survived the ravages of time. There were many more before the Nazi Blitz leveled large sections of historic London, but even before then, the spot has a long and rather grim history. It was a focal point of grief in the neighborhood during the Black Death of 1348 when the field just outside the gates was used as a mass grave. The Black Death, a form of plague, killed off a third of Europe's population and London was by no means spared. The field where an estimated 55,000 dead were hastily buried is now a paved-over square, but to this day nothing has been built on it.

The Charterhouse today

Next to this field, Sir Walter de Manny built a Carthusian monastery in 1371, which became an important religious institution for the rest of the Middle Ages up to the Tudor period. That all changed when King Henry VIII broke from Rome and installed himself as the head of the new Church of England. The monks rejected this change, wanting to stay loyal to Rome. In typical fashion, Henry came down hard on them, and their prior, John Houghton, was hanged, drawn, and quartered. As if that wasn't enough to prove his point, Henry ordered that one of his arms be nailed to the door of the monastery to serve as a warning against any further resistance.

It did not have the intended effect. Ghosts of long-dead monks began to appear in the monastery at night, beseeching their living brethren to stay true to Rome. Henry executed eighteen more monks and still, they did not waver. At last, Henry ordered the monastery disbanded, as he had with so many other religious houses throughout the land, and the building was given to Lord North, who refurbished it into a private home.

In 1611, the building was purchased by Sir Thomas Sutton, one of the richest men in London, who turned it into a charitable foundation. Part of the property was set aside as a hospital for elderly men. According to Sutton's will, they had to be "either decrepit or old captains either at sea or at land, maimed or disabled soldiers, merchants fallen on hard times, those ruined by shipwreck or other calamity." Another part was a school for poor boys.

Charterhouse remains one of the most prestigious of London's private charities. Wellington, Gladstone, and Cromwell have all served as Governors, and it has been used in scenes in works by Daniel Defoe, Charles Dickens, and William Thackeray. Thackeray, who grew up poor, attended the Charterhouse school, as did Robert Baden-Powell and John Wesley. While the school has since moved to another location, the Charterhouse remains a home for elderly men, who are called "Brothers."

It also remains a home for the ghosts of loyal monks who have long since stopped speaking with the living. Having been defeated by the advance of Protestantism, one remains behind, woefully wandering the medieval courtyards at night, mourning the loss of his beloved monastery. Another ghost is that of Thomas Howard, 4th Duke of Norfolk, who was arrested in the Charterhouse for plotting against Queen Elizabeth and later beheaded at the Tower of London. He is sometimes seen at night, descending the main staircase, holding his head in his hands.

The 4th Duke of Norfolk

In early 2017, the Charterhouse was opened to the public for the first time, and people can walk through the medieval courtyard and sumptuous interiors. Tours are led by one of the Brothers.

An equally interesting London attraction is the Handel House Museum at 25 Brook Street in

Mayfair. This is where the famous composer, George Frideric Handel, lived and worked for 36 years until he died in his bedroom upstairs in 1759. Now, the lovely Georgian home has been converted into a museum in his memory, holding regular concerts in one of the rooms.

Handel

The building had been a private residence for many years until it was purchased in 2000 by the Handel House Trust and opened as a museum the following year. During the painstaking restoration, the trustees discovered they had purchased more than they had bargained for when several workmen saw the faint apparition of a woman. Even one of the trust's fundraisers, Martin Egglestone, twice spotted the spirit. The first time, he was measuring some curtains when he felt the air grow thick and heavy and he saw a bright shape before his eyes, which he described as looking like an afterimage left on the retina after staring at a bright light source. The image slowly coalesced into the vague form of a woman floating above him. Although startled, Egglestone did not feel threatened by the ghost.

Others working on the building smelled the strong odor of perfume in the upstairs bedroom. They theorize this might be the lingering scent of two rival sopranos, Faustina Bordoni and Francesca Cuzzoni, who competed for Handel's favor.

In July of 2001, the trustees called in a priest to investigate the matter. He came to the same conclusions as the trustees, that the ghost was not malevolent and should be helped to find peace in this world and the next.

The Most Haunted House in London

THE "HAUNTED HOUSE," BERKELEY SQUARE.

While the controversy continues over whether the Borley Rectory was or was not haunted, another home has taken on the mantle of the "Most Haunted House in London." Number 50 Berkeley Square is an unassuming Late Georgian period townhouse in London's high-end neighborhood of Mayfair. Berkeley Square certainly doesn't look like the typical place for a haunting—it's a beautiful square set away from the hustle and bustle of London's busier financial and shopping districts. Here, there are homes and quieter offices for various financial companies. Laid out in the middle of the 18th century, it has a fine garden that, unlike many others in London's finer districts, is open to the public. One can relax on the grass and admire the tall Plane trees, planted shortly after the square had been laid out.

It appears that trouble first began at the house in the late 19th century after a hundred years of peace. Perhaps no one had yet died in the house who wished to stay on this Earth. The restless spirit may be one of the famous former residents. Prime Minister George Canning lived there until his death in 1827. While he was, by far, the most famous person to have owned the house, the other owners tended to be important figures of the day in their own right.

Canning

In 1859, a Mr. Myers moved in. It was then that the hauntings began, or at least, the first manifestations to be recorded for posterity. This was already the scientific age and many people no longer believed in ghosts. To report one tended to invite ridicule.

Mr. Myers reported plenty of ghosts and things started to go badly for him in a very mundane way. He was engaged to be married and spent a large amount of money fitting out the house to his fiancé's expectations only for her to jilt him at the last minute. Falling into a deep depression, Myers became a recluse. He no longer maintained his house, saw no one, and lived only in a small servants quarters on the top floor. He would never answer the door except when a servant, who did not live at the property, came to bring him food. Neighbors could sometimes see Myers wandering the house at night, lighting his way with a single candle. Occasionally, they heard strange sounds and babbling emanating from the lonely home. Myers never stepped outside, and what little details his neighbors could glean from the servant indicated that he had gone mad. The property gradually fell into decay—the windows were never washed, the soot was never scrubbed from the walls, and what could be seen of the interior through the windows looked tattered and covered with dust.

Rumors began to circulate that Myers wasn't the only being wandering the house at night.

When he was brought to court in 1873 for failure to pay his council tax, the magistrate let him off due to the fact that he had lived in "the haunted house," an unusual way to dodge taxes if ever there was one. He died the next year, with his taxes still unpaid.

Later residents of the house reported that the hauntings were centered around the same room in which Myers had lived, but strangely, most stories said it was not the spirit of the jilted bachelor who had been causing the trouble. The attic room where Myers had spent his lonely vigil mourning his love life was apparently the scene of a suicide. Sometime before Myers had moved in, a young women supposedly hanged herself there after having been molested by her uncle. She is said to appear as a ghostly white figure or occasionally a brown mist. A variant of the tale says it was of a young girl who had been killed by her servant.

Either way, the ghost was a terrifying one that was ultimately responsible for killing more than one witness. In 1879, *Mayfair Magazine* reported that a maid who didn't know the story of the haunted room had taken up residence there. One night, ear-splitting screams rang through the house. When the owners ran up to the servant's quarters to investigate, they found the maid in a frenzy, babbling about having seen a ghost. She could not be calmed down and was sent to an asylum, where she died of heart failure the next day, literally scared to death.

By this time, the upstairs room had developed quite a reputation. George William Lyttelton, the 4th Baron Lyttelton, offered to stay in the haunted room. Unlike many people who had boasted they weren't afraid of haunted houses and offered to stay in them overnight, Lyttelton was not a doubter. He stayed in the room not to disprove the ghost, but to prove his own bravery, strengthening his courage by bringing his trusty shotgun along. Around the middle of the night, the ghostly girl appeared. In shock, Lyttelton fired at it, proving chivalry is dead when it came to the dead.

A contemporary sketch depicting Lyttelton

The next day, Lyttelton investigated the attic with the aid of daylight but could find no trace of the ghost. He was sure he had hit it since he had fired with a shotgun at point-blank range, but there was no trace of blood, only the scattering of the shot on the opposite wall. Whatever he had seen that night, it had been no human hoaxer.

Had the house been haunted before Myers had become a recluse? In his depression, had he gained some sick satisfaction sleeping in a haunted room and keeping company with a ghost who was just as unhappy as he was? Did his own disinterest in life give him immunity to the terror of seeing the ghost? Whatever the truth of the tale, both Myers and the ghost have moved on, and there haven't been any reported hauntings at 50 Berkeley Square for a couple of generations.

Haunted Churches and Cemeteries

St. Paul's Cathedral isn't the only historic church to be haunted. In fact, many historic churches continue to be visited by the spirits of dead priests and parishioners.

St. Giles on Camberwell High Street is one such site. Although the present church opened in 1844—little more than yesterday, given London's history—there has been a church there for almost a thousand years. It is mentioned in the *Domesday Book*, that great Norman census of their newly conquered lands finished in 1086. Back then, when the area was a village, the book lists "22 villagers and 7 small-holders with land for 6 ploughs…a church, 63 acres of meadow and woodland providing 60 pigs." Now, at the center of a booming metropolis, the church and churchyard still emit an atmosphere of tranquility and peace.

Historians believe this has always been a magical place. The Old English "Camberwell" translates as "crooked well." St. Giles is the patron saint of people with physical disabilities, leading many to believe it had once been the site of a holy well where people came, hoping to be healed. Such wells were common throughout England in ancient and medieval times. Many were originally sacred springs of Pagan deities before being Christianized in the early Middle Ages. By the turn of the last century, many had fallen into disuse, but holy wells are seeing a resurgence today, as some English people, dissatisfied with mass commercialization and the loss of the past, are seeking a closer connection with their roots.

Visitors to St. Giles can experience one of these connections to the past in the form of a phantom priest. Next to the church is a narrow path called the Churchyard Passage that goes around the western side of the church and through the old cemetery before it ends. It used to finish at the Clergy House, home of the resident priest, but that building disappeared long ago. In the 1930s and 40s, it was common for visitors to the graveyard to see a priest walking along the Churchyard Passage. Unlike some of the ghosts in this study, no one ever felt any fear at the sight of this ghostly clergyman. Rather, church workers have grown accustomed to him. The priest always seems happy and at peace, linked to this earth, not because of some great tragedy, but out of love for his old church and home.

Like many ghosts, the kindly old priest has faded over the years. By the 1970s, he had become a mere shadow, barely discernable as a man at all, yet he still appeared regularly and was even written up in the church magazine where several parishioners wrote about their own experiences. The priest hasn't been seen in years, and one might wonder if he finally left this earth or if some faint trace of him continues his walk down the old Churchyard Passage.

St. Mary's Church on Neasden Lane is another old church, founded in 938 by King Athelstan.

Popularly called St. Mary's Willesden, it was famous in the Middle Ages as a pilgrimage destination for those who sought the Virgin Mary's intercession. The oldest parts of the present church date to the 13th century.

Back then, pilgrimages weren't the somber affairs they are so often today. Rather, they were a chance to see distant friends, drink a lot, and maybe have an affair with a friendly stranger. Father Donald, who preached at St. Paul's Cross in London around the year 1350, railed against the naughty pilgrims, saying, "Ye men of London, gangen [go] yourselves with your wives to Wilsdon in the devil's name, or else keep them at home with you in sorrow!"

The resident ghost haunts the vicarage garden and has been seen by many people. He is said to be a jovial, fat, little monk. He is most often seen around what some believe to have been a holy, old well. Linguists say that in Old English, "Wellesden" means a spring or well at the foot of a hill, hinting at a holy well on the site. Unusually for a ghost, the monk sometimes appears at noon as well as at dawn and dusk. Perhaps the monk got fat off of all the good food and drink the pilgrims enjoyed.

Strange phenomena have been reported inside the church, as well. Sometimes, visitors catch a strong whiff of incense when none is burning, and the vestry door handle rattles when no one is there. Whether this is the same spirit as the one in the garden is not known.

Another haunted church is the appropriately named All Hallows Barking—also known as All Hallows by the Tower—on Byward Street. This church is one of the oldest in London, having been founded in 675 during the Anglo-Saxon era. A small part of the original structure can still be seen, although much of it was restored after being badly damaged in the Blitz. It is haunted by a harmless spirit who loves church music.

Ben Brooksbank's picture of the church after being damaged by German bombing

The church today

This spirit was first brought to public attention by the choirmaster and two choir boys, who were practicing after hours in the church one cold December evening in 1920. They were getting ready for the Christmas service that would take place in a few days and had locked the church so they wouldn't be disturbed. As the boys sang, they were surprised to see an old woman standing and watching them with great interest. She was wearing clothing a generation out of date in fashion and had sallow, drawn features. Thinking it impolite to ask who she was and how she had managed to get inside, one of the boys fetched her a chair. She nodded her thanks and sat down. The boys and the choir leader continued with their practice as the woman eagerly watched.

As the trio continued their practice, their minds raced with the mystery of this woman. They couldn't figure out how she had gotten inside or why they hadn't heard her footsteps on the flagstones as she approached. None of them recognized her as one of the regulars of the church. The mystery only deepened when they finished their last song. As the last note faded away in the echoing interior of the church, the woman vanished. A moment later, they heard a scratching against one of the walls, as if a cat was trying to get out of the building. Then, one of the boys saw a cat rush down the south aisle. Thoroughly baffled, the choirmaster and the two boys searched the entire church but could find no trace of either the old woman or the cat.

And there the mystery rested for a time, until five years later, when the choirmaster was approached by an old man whom he had never seen before. It turned out the boys had talked about their experience, and word had spread. He told the choirmaster that he knew the identity of the ghost. He had been a choirboy himself at the same church sixty years before, and one of the regular attendees had been an eccentric old woman who had loved cats and church music in equal measure. She'd kept countless cats at home and fed every stray cat in the neighborhood. She had such a reputation with London's felines that a crowd of them would follow her wherever she went, even to church. She loved carols and would pay the boys to walk with her through the district singing them.

The old cat- and carol-loving lady was seen quite frequently in All Hallows Church throughout the 1920s and 1930s but has since faded away.

Haunted Pubs

It's no secret Londoners like to unwind with a drink or two. Friday and Saturday nights can get pretty rowdy, and visitors to the city should take care. But there are also allegedly some unseen drunks that hang around London's many pubs.

Perhaps the most haunted pub is the Grenadier, hidden in Wilton Mews in the district of Belgravia. The building was erected in 1720, close to an army barracks. The upper story served as the officers' mess while the cellar was a lowly drinking and gambling den for privates.

One September night, a young subaltern thought he might cheat the privates at cards. He wasn't as clever as he thought he was, however. The enlisted men caught him in the act, beating him so badly he was laid up in the hospital for several days before dying, probably from internal injuries.

Ever since then, the building has been haunted by the spirit of this unlucky man. It became a pub in 1818, first named the Guardsmen after the soldiers nearby and then renamed the Grenadier in honor of the heroic actions of the Grenadier Guards at the Battle of Waterloo. Indeed, the victorious general of that battle, the Duke of Wellington, used to drink there. King George IV was also a patron. The soldiers have long since gone, but the ghost has stayed on. He is most often seen in September, the month he was killed, and appears as the faint image of a somber man in military dress, walking without a sound through the building. Sometimes he isn't seen, but felt with a sudden plunge in temperature that lingers for days no matter how much the landlord turns up the central heating. Other times, objects disappear only to reappear in a completely different part of the building. Drinkers and staff alike have seen furniture rattle when no one was nearby.

One odd event happened to the chief superintendent of New Scotland Yard when he was having a drink and noticed wisps of smoke coming from an unseen source beside him. Curious, he began to feel around for the source of the smoke when an invisible cigarette burned his hand.

Head barman, Greyam Fox, who worked at the pub in 1982 and 1983 was in the habit of leaving a lit cigarette in an ashtray in the cellar storeroom during the busy hours when he didn't have time for a cigarette break, but that didn't stop a determined smoker like Fox. He left the cigarette in the storeroom since he had to duck in there on a regular basis, anyway. When he did, he'd take a couple of quick puffs and fetch whatever it was he had gone for. His boss and the patrons were none the wiser.

The ghost was onto his game, however, and one night when he rushed in there to take a drag, he noticed the landlord's black cat, Bobby, had somehow gotten out of the private rooms upstairs and made its way, unseen, down to the cellar. Fox thought it odd, and as he stared at the cat and picking up his cigarette, the cat arched its back, hissed, and latched onto Fox's leg with its teeth and claws. At the same moment, the ashtray lifted into the air, flew against the wall, and smashed into a dozen pieces. The temperature plunged, as well. Fox fled in terror and never again stayed in the cellar any longer than he had to.

Another haunted cellar exists beneath the Viaduct Tavern, established in the Victorian era as a gin palace in 1869, the opening of which showed a change in attitude toward the drink. Gin—usually badly made and responsible for many cases of alcohol poisoning, blindness, and dementia—had been the scourge of the 18th century. Even the well-made stuff was so strong and addictive that many people lost their livelihood through their addiction to drink. In 1751, William Hogarth made a famous print called *Gin Lane*, showing a gin-soaked crowd fighting, committing suicide, hawking their worldly possessions, and neglecting their children. Hogarth felt beer was a far finer drink, and his accompanying print, *Beer Street,* shows happy, healthy tipplers in a prosperous neighborhood.

In the face of death from drink, the government finally stepped in and instituted quality laws on gin. By the 19th century Victorian era, when the Viaduct opened, gin had become respectable again. Instead of going to seedy little "dram shops," now people could drink at elegantly decorated "gin palaces."

The Viaduct is the only remaining Victorian gin palace, still serving the many barristers who work at the Old Bailey across the street. Previously, on the site of the Old Bailey was the notorious Newgate Prison, torn down in 1902. Prisoners condemned to die were led along "Dead Man's Walk," between the prison and the court. Local tradition says the water fountain across the street from where the pub stands today is where the prisoners were hanged.

While its public areas are warm, friendly, and respectable, the Viaduct's cellar is another matter. It's a grim place, divided into five sections that some historians say are original Newgate cells. Others say that the walls were, in fact, cells from the debtors' prison, Giltspur Compter, which supposedly stood on the spot until 1853. Others dismiss these ideas, claiming they are nothing more than storerooms.

Wherever the truth lies, something isn't quite right about that cellar. Staff members swear it's the den of a poltergeist. Numerous workers have seen objects move on their own and heard strange sounds down there. One day in 1996, the manager went into the cellar to tidy up when the lights switched off, and the door slammed shut. He managed to fumble back to the door but found that while he was able to turn the knob, he was unable to pull it open. Thoroughly frightened, he called to his wife to help. When she got downstairs, she was able to open the door with ease.

Three years later, two electricians were in the process of fixing the wiring upstairs. To get at the wires, they had to roll the carpet up, set it to one side, and take up the floorboards. As they did so, one of the workmen felt a tap on his shoulder. He turned to his colleague, but the man said he hadn't done it. He felt the tap a few more times, and the electrician was beginning to think his chum was playing a rather childish trick, when the rolled-up carpet lifted into the air and fell back onto the floor with a thump.

Another historic pub is the Flask, an 18th-century tavern in Highgate. It was a favorite of artist William Hogarth, who once sketched a bar fight there when two drunks started clubbing one another with their tankards, demonstrating how a true artist can find inspiration in anything.

One strange detail of this pub is a bullet embedded in the wall to the right of the front door with a strange tale to tell. Local legend says the bullet was fired during a bar fight, missed its target, and passed through the body of a young barmaid, killing her instantly. Others say she committed suicide after she was jilted by her secret lover.

The phantom barmaid doesn't appear often, but when she does, she always causes a sensation.

First, the temperature in the pub suddenly goes down, the ceiling lights slowly start to sway, and glasses slide across the tables. Some patrons even feel her cold breath down their necks.

A more lighthearted spirit—one that has the annoying habit of flushing the toilet when someone is sitting on it—dwells in the ladies' room at the Bow Bells on Bow Street. Despite many irate ladies complaining of splashed bottoms and numerous plumbers being called in to fix the loo, the problem continues.

Sometimes, the phantom is seen as a thick mist rising from the bar late at night. Back in 1974, the landlord decided to hold a séance to communicate with the annoying prankster from beyond. The only response he got was when the toilet door slammed shut so hard, the frosted glass pane on it smashed to pieces. Since then, successive landlords have decided to respect the ghost's privacy, even if it doesn't respect the privacy of the female patrons.

Underground Ghosts

The London Underground opened its first line in 1863. The world's first underground railway system, it was hailed as a modern marvel, and remains one of the world's busiest systems, carrying well over a billion people a year.

It is also believed to have ghosts.

Several of the stations are haunted. At Aldgate Station—one of the oldest stations, having opened in 1876—hauntings are so frequent that they've even made it into the official station log. The control room is situated on an older rail line which intersects with the present line. There, engineers have heard footsteps passing over the sleepers and stopping where there used to be a door. Some think this might be the spirit of a former engineer who hasn't realized the floor plan of the station has changed. Sometimes, late at night, engineers hear a ghostly whistling echoing down the tunnels.

One day in the late 1960s, an engineer was working on the conductor rail, surprised to see a colleague pass by with an old woman who was gently stroking his hair. The woman wasn't an employee. Even stranger, the worker did not seem to notice her. Before the witness could react, the worker made a mistake with the electric lines, sending 22,000 volts surging through his body. He was knocked out cold but suffered no other ill effects. To be electrocuted by that high of a voltage and not die is a minor miracle in and of itself.

Over at Bank Station, there's the spirit of the Black Nun. The station gets its name from being situated right next to the Bank of England. The name of this particular ghost is known, which is unusual for ghosts. The spirit is that of Sarah Whitehead, though she is not actually a nun. Rather, she is a woman wearing the black dress and veil of mourning. Back in the early 19th century, her brother, who had worked at the bank, was charged with forgery. Justice was rougher in those days, and he was executed for the crime. The Whitehead family knew that Sarah and her brother had been close and that Sarah had a delicate constitution, so they didn't tell her about her brother's trial, imprisonment, or execution.

Baffled and hurt by her brother's disappearance, Sarah kept going to the Bank of England to ask after him. At first, they put her off with various excuses or by saying they didn't know where he was, but her visits became so frequent that one clerk finally broke the silence and angrily told her that her brother had been a thief, was hanged for his crimes, and that she should never come back.

This did not end her visits. Sarah's mind snapped, and she kept going back to the bank day after day, forlornly asking after her brother. The bank directors took pity on her and gave her a remittance. When she died, she was buried in a private garden close to the bank, but even that did not stop her visits. Now, she is frequently encountered on nearby Threadneedle Street, sometimes in broad daylight, asking passersby if they have seen her brother. She also descends into nearby Bank Station to ask commuters the same thing. Sarah is always seen in her mourning clothes. Her face, only vaguely seen through the black veil, wears the stricken look of pure grief.

Covent Garden Station, one of London's busiest, also has a busy ghost that has been seen dozens of times. Jack Hayden, a traveling inspector, was first to see it in the 1950s while sitting in the underground mess room, filling out some paperwork on Christmas Eve. He heard the door rattle, called out that it was not a public area, and opened the door to give the traveler directions. The inspector was startled to see a tall man floating down the nearby spiral staircase, wearing a Homburg-style hat, long out of fashion and tight trousers.

Since then, workers have seen the same figure in various parts of the station, always wearing the same strange clothes and floating a bit off the floor. Even the station foreman saw him twice. He logged the incident, noting the dates as the 24th and 27th of March 1972.

The ghost has been tentatively identified—based on his appearance and the style of his clothing—as Victorian actor William Terriss, a stage favorite who was murdered in 1897 by a fellow actor in a fit of jealousy. The murderer had felt overshadowed by Terriss' success and believed his more famous colleague was deliberately holding back his career. Terriss was in the habit of taking the Tube to work at the Adelphi Theatre, getting off at Covent Garden, the nearest station.

Terriss

While ghosts tend to be seen late at night in remote locations by only one or two witnesses, the spirit that haunts King's Cross Station has been seen in the middle of the day by large crowds. She's a young woman with long brown hair, simply dressed in jeans and a t-shirt in the style of the 1980s who is seen in various parts of the station, sobbing uncontrollably. When people gather to comfort her and ask what's wrong, she suddenly vanishes. At other times, in the wee hours of the morning, when the station is closed and only the custodians are there, her mournful cries echo around the empty station.

She is believed to be one of 31 victims of a terrible fire that broke out in 1987 when a lit match dropped on an escalator ignited some grease beneath the steps. The fire smoldered for a time before flaring up. At that time, the escalator had steps made of wood and soon caught fire, trapping hundreds in the lower area of the station as it filled with smoke.

An even worse disaster befell Bethnal Green Station in East London during World War Two. It was 1943, and the Luftwaffe had been bombing London almost every night. Air raid sirens went off regularly. Sometimes they were false alarms, sometimes tests, but more often they were the real thing. Whenever the sirens started to blare, everyone made for their nearest air raid shelter. Tube stations were a favorite refuge since they were deeper and sturdier than regular cellars, thus offering better protection.

One day, the air raid siren went off, and Londoners near the entrance to Bethnal Green station hurried to the entrance. Then tragedy struck. By some trick of the movement of the crowd, too many people converged on the entrance at the same time. Someone tripped and those hurrying behind tripped over him or her. This led to a chain reaction and soon, a large portion of the crowd was stumbling down the stairs, crushing those in front. A total of 173 people died in the crush, including 41 children.

Today, late at night, staff and the last travelers of the evening have heard the sound of crying children and screaming women. Others have felt the suffocating sensation of closeness, much like what those poor souls must have felt in their final moments.

Over in East London, another tragedy spurred a haunting. Becontree Station is actually an aboveground station, but is part of the London Underground, being a stop on the District Line. On January 30, 1958, two trains left the station just minutes before being accidentally shunted onto the same line. The second train was moving faster and collided into the back of the first one, derailing it. 10 people were killed and 93 were injured. Now, the pale, white figure of a woman is sometimes seen at the end of the platform, looking down the line in the direction of the crash. Several have seen her figure and felt a strange foreboding about her. In 1992, a station supervisor came face to face with this entity, in a manner of speaking. He was doing some paperwork one night when he heard the door to his office rattle. When he opened the door, no one was there.

The man left the office, feeling somewhat unsettled, and started up the stairs to the platform. He remembers having a sudden terror of being alone and the impulse to find someone to stand near. He had a terrible feeling that someone was following him, and he kept looking over his shoulder to reassure himself that he was alone. Then, he looked back once too many times. Right behind him stood a woman in a white dress. She looked young and had blonde hair. Her face, however, was a complete blank—there were no eyes, no nose, and no mouth. The vision slowly faded away. When the terrified supervisor rushed to find the nearest staff member on duty, he was told that many of the station workers had seen the apparition and grown accustomed to it.

Ickenham Station on the Metropolitan and Piccadilly Lines is haunted by a strange woman who has appeared to numerous members of the staff. The first sighting was at 2 a.m. in March of 1951. A London Transport engineer working the late shift at a sub-station on one end of one of the platforms looked up and noticed middle-aged woman watching him from some distance away. She looked real. The engineer also noticed the red scarf she wore around her head. The woman moved to a large switchboard and beckoned him to follow. He was curious, so he did. The woman, who hadn't uttered a word, descended a nearby staircase, vanishing as she got to the bottom. It was only then the engineer realized he had been following a ghost.

Since that night, several London Transport employees working late at night have seen the ghost. They believe it to be the spirit of a woman who died when she fell on the conductor rail many decades ago.

Room 333: The Haunted Hotel Room

For those staying in London as visitors, it would be good to remember that they might not be the only inhabitant in the hotel room. Several of the city's historic hotels contain the spirits of former guests.

Of all the hotels, the Langham in Marylebone is the most haunted. Opened in 1865, the five-star hotel is popular with wealthy tourists and business travelers. Several ghosts haunt its rooms and corridors. The most persistent ghost inhabits room 333, which has gained the dubious distinction of the being city's most haunted hotel room.

The Langham

The ghost is that of a man dressed in Victorian period eveningwear. It is said the man had killed his wife in the room before taking his own life. Now, he often appears to those who stay there. James Alexander Gordon, a BBC sports broadcaster, saw the phantom in 1973. Gordon described the ghost as a bright ball of light that appeared suddenly and slowly took the form of a man missing his legs below the knees. The apparition hovered there for a moment, staring at Gordon, then glided through the air, opening his arms as if to embrace him. Perhaps not surprisingly, Gordon ran out of the room and spent the night elsewhere.

Other ghosts at the Langham include a German prince clad in military attire, reputed to have thrown himself out of an upper story window at the outbreak of World War I. It is said he loved England so much he couldn't bear to become its enemy. Thus, he remains in England for all time, hovering near the window from which he plunged to his death. As well, guests on the third floor are often stopped by the specter of a dead butler who is still trying to do his job long after his demise.

There's also Napoleon III, one of the hotel's many famous guests, who is said to lurk in the basement. Why a French emperor would lurk in such a mundane area of the hotel remains a mystery.

In 2014, several members of the English cricket team staying at the hotel for the London test matches suffered strange experiences. Stuart Broad complained the taps in his bathroom would turn on and wake him up. As soon as he turned the lights on, they'd switch off but come on again when he switched the lights off. Other players were awoken with the sense they were not alone in the room, although they could see no one there. Several members requested room changes, and many of the players' wives and girlfriends refused to stay with them.

Just Plain Weird

Some ghost sightings defy explanation, even among the credulous ranks of ghost hunters. Perhaps the strangest ghost to be seen at night in London is that of a chicken who met an untimely end at the hands of one of the nation's greatest early scientists. This odd apparition can sometimes be seen in Pond Square in Highgate. There's nothing remarkable about Pond Square, an upper-class neighborhood with a small garden and trees at its center. It gets its name from the two ponds that were there until they were filled in 1864. Many ponds and streams of old London were filled in or covered up in the 18th and 19th centuries, and spiritualists say that places with subterranean water often act as magnets for paranormal phenomena.

It was on this site in the 16th century that Sir Francis Bacon made his home. Bacon (1561-1626) was a leading figure of his day, holding various political posts throughout his eventful life, most notably that of Attorney General and Lord Chancellor. It was his contribution to scientific knowledge, however, that has brought him lasting fame. He was one of the first English scientists to advocate the scientific method, saying that the only way to gain true insight into nature was to use inductive reasoning and experimentation in order to find answers to scientific questions. It was the same method that sadly led to his demise. One of his theories was that meat could be preserved in cool temperatures. While this seems obvious today, in the age before electricity and modern gadgets, animals were slaughtered only hours or minutes before being cooked. Bacon knew that if meat could be preserved at low temperatures, it would revolutionize how food was stored and distributed. He decided to test his theory in March of 1626, when he bought a hen from a local vendor, killed it, plucked it, and stuffed it with ice to see if it would slow its decay. In the process, Bacon, unfortunately, caught a chill. His cold grew worse, and he was given the guest room at his friend, Lord Arundel's, house to recover. The room was damp and musty, as many rooms are in London to this day. Even the bed on which he lay was damp. Sir Bacon's cold grew worse until he developed pneumonia. The great scientist and statesman died on April 9.

Bacon

That was the end of Sir Francis Bacon, but not the chicken. Ever since, unlucky pedestrians in Pond Square on dark nights have seen the ghost of a chicken. It appears out of nowhere, minus its head and feathers, and runs around in circles, flapping its wings before disappearing into thin air. The appearances were so regular that it became something of a local legend. Sightings continued well into the 20th century. In 1943, Terrence Long was crossing the square late one night when he heard the sound of a horse-drawn carriage rumbling over the cobblestones. He looked around, thinking he might witness a phantom carriage, a popular apparition in Britain when instead, he was amazed to see Sir Bacon's dead chicken carrying out its usual routine of running around the square and vanishing. Why it was accompanied by the sound of a horse and carriage has never been explained.

Another rude awakening came in the 1970s when a young couple took advantage of the darkness in the shade of the trees to have a little bit of fun. Just as their passion had reached its peak, the headless, featherless chicken dropped down on them from above. It was certainly a rude ending to their date, and one can only hope the chicken sighting didn't ruin their relationship.

These days, the Ghost Chicken of Pond Square isn't seen much anymore. Perhaps it has finally found peace, forgiven its murderer, and joined Sir Francis Bacon in that great dining room in the sky.

The headless chicken isn't the only phantom to make physical contact with unsuspecting Londoners. There's also the strange case of a ghostly arm reported in April of 1907. In that year, a letter was sent to the *City Press* newspaper: "On Sunday night, while walking home down London Wall [Street], I passed by the old piece of 'London Wall' which is railed off from the road. Suddenly I was aware of a hand, and arm stretched out from the railings to bar my passage. Being scared, I jumped off the pavement into the road, and for a moment turned my back to the railings. On looking round, I saw a man dressed in dark clothes, walking back to the wall. He was wearing no hat when he reached the wall, and seemed to walk right into it. I could hear no sound of steps, and on close investigation after he had disappeared I could see no man and no hole in the wall. I went on Monday to look at the place, and I cannot throw any light on the subject. Possibly some of your readers have seen the same thing. I shall be very interested to hear if they have."

The London Wall is a stretch of the old defensive wall that surrounded "the City," what is now the financial district but was previously the extent of Roman Londinium and the medieval city of London. While most of the wall dates from the medieval period, the Roman foundations are visible in many spots. Nowadays it's a bustling area, with the modern Museum of London overlooking the best-preserved section of the wall.

A statue of Trajan in front of the ruins of the Roman wall in London

Travelers at night in London need to beware. Not only are there violent drunks, ghostly chickens, and phantom arms to contend with, but there's even a ghost bus. It's seen along Cambridge Gardens in central London, just a little northwest of Marble Arch. It's said to be an old-style, double-decker, a number 7. The bus route still runs through the area. The bus was first spotted in 1934, when a driver, who was going along Cambridge Gardens in the early hours of the morning, suddenly swerved and crashed. The man died, and witnesses said they could see no reason why he would have swerved. He had been driving normally up until then, and there was nothing in his way. At the inquest, however, several local residents came forward to tell a strange tale. They had all seen a ghostly bus pass along the street at or around 1:15 a.m., the exact time of the crash. They said the bus had no lights on, no driver was visible, and that it sped down the center of the road, forcing anyone driving on Cambridge Garden to swerve out of the way. Several motorists have sworn they had seen the bus and had to pull hard on the wheel to avoid it. When they looked in the rearview mirror, however, the road was empty. Had this phantom bus finally caused a fatal accident?

There's also the strange tale of the phantom breakfast, taking place in the fine old Georgian building at 7 Park Road at Regents Park. The dining room was originally the kitchen, but back in the middle of the 20th century, a new set of owners converted the old, outdated kitchen into a dining room, moving the kitchen elsewhere. Despite having taken out the giant, black iron range, and all other fittings, painting the walls, and putting in new furniture, the room remained the kitchen, as far as the spirits were concerned. In the mornings, residents detect the rich smell of coffee and bacon pervading the room and reaching up to the story above. Even after the building had been converted to a dentist's office, the smells could still be detected.

Parapsychologists and occultists believe ghosts are tied to places of importance to them in life, like those poor souls killed in the panic at Bethnal Green Station or the Duke of Norfolk who was arrested on the stairs of the Charterhouse. Ghost hunters point to the famous London Bridge as proof of this theory. There has been a bridge at the same spot since Roman times, rebuilt several times due to various tragedies. The early medieval wooden bridge was the site for the execution of condemned witches. The bridge was replaced with a stone one in 1209 but caused many fatalities thanks to having narrow arches causing the river to flow in rapids underneath. This caused several crashes and capsizings of boats on the Thames.

The stone bridge was more than simply a way to cross the river. Houses and shops were built-up on both sides, so the way across became quite narrow. These ramshackle wooden buildings rose up to seven stories. Everyone thought it was a good place to own a business or live until a fire sadly broke out in 1212. In fact, both ends caught fire. How this could have happened is unclear. Perhaps an arsonist set fire to the bridge, or maybe it was an irate witch getting vengeance for her fallen sisters. Whatever happened, it was one of London's worst disasters, with some 3,000 people being trapped on the bridge as the fire quickly spread. An unknown number of people succumbed to the smoke and flames or drowned as they dove into the river below.

The stone bridge survived, but that did not end its grisly history. When witches were no longer hanged upon its span, the heads of executed criminals were stuck on pikes at the southern end of the bridge to warn potential criminals that justice prevailed in London. William Wallace, Sir Thomas More, and Guy Fawkes all suffered this fate.

When a new London Bridge was built in 1831, it was put in the same place as the previous bridges and used some of the earlier foundations. It is not the one people see in London today because that one was purchased by American developers in the 1960s and removed to Lake Havasu, Arizona, where it was rebuilt stone by stone. Reopened in 1971, it spans the lake and makes for an unusual landmark in that popular vacation and retirement spot.

The bridge isn't the only thing the American developers brought over. It appears the spirits of the bridge have also come along. Even on its day of inauguration, several ghosts made their appearance in the form of four people in Elizabethan garb walking along the bridge. Thinking they were part of the dedication ceremony, a woman pointed them out to her friends. Just as they spotted them, they disappeared. Ever since, there has been a spate of ghost sightings on the bridge, following the same pattern: someone sees one or more individuals in historic costume who vanish as soon as they are approached.

Not only do ghosts attach themselves to particular places, but to particular objects as well. In the wig room of the Victoria Palace Theatre, there dwells a very peculiar ghost. Many actors and crew have seen wigs fly across the room, and the door locks and unlocks seemingly at random. No one has an explanation for this phenomenon, but it certainly makes the actors get in and get out of the wig room as quickly as possible.

More ominous is the strange tale of Sotiris Charalambous and Joseph Birch, two young flatmates who found a fine old walnut mirror in a skip—what Americans would call a dumpster. Puzzled that someone would throw away such a good home accessory, they brought it home to Muswell Hill, painted the frame silver, and hung it up in the living room. That was when the trouble started. They both started having terrible nightmares, thinking they were being attacked and awoke to find scratches on their bodies. Both habitually trimmed their nails short so they couldn't have done it to themselves, nor were they responsible for the sensation of being stabbed that woke them up almost every night.

Things grew worse, and the sleep-deprived friends started seeing shadows in the mirror. They were never distinct, but they were certainly not reflections of shadows in the room. The flat was also subjected to a spate of poltergeist activity, including moving or disappearing objects, things falling over, and the radiator and telephone line breaking.

Deciding someone had been murdered in front of the mirror, they decided to get rid of it on eBay and managed to sell it for £100. Maybe the mirror had captured the reflection of a foul crime along with the victim's spirit, or maybe the flat mates simply made up the story to grab attention on eBay.

Perhaps the most disturbing haunting of all is located at the Cane Hill Lunatic Asylum in Croydon. The asylum first opened in 1883 and operated until 1992, when it finally closed its doors forever. Generations of the mentally ill lived there in their private hell. In the early years, mental health care was primitive, and the patients' conditions were often made worse by the liberal use of straight-jackets, cold water baths, and isolation. Charlie Chaplin's mother was there for a time, although once the great comedian had earned success on the silver screen, he found her a better place in private care. The brothers of David Bowie and Michael Caine have also been patients at Cane Hill, although by then the standards of care had much improved.

Hywell Williams' picture of the asylum in 2005 after it had closed

Ever since it closed, rumors that the spirits of some of the tortured souls remain at the derelict building. Dog walkers find that their pets shy away if they try to lead them close to the building, and those who brave a closer look have been known to see shadows move across the open windows.

Like any empty building with a storied past, it has attracted its share of partiers, urban explorers, and ghost hunters. Because of this, the National Health Service posted a security team—who have experienced several strange phenomena—to keep trespassers out. In a particularly frightening incident, a guard was going around with his guard dog—an aggressive brute and one of the few animals that would dare to step onto the property—when the dog started barking furiously at a patch of woodland next to the old asylum. The guard let the dog off its lead to pursue the intruder, but instead, the dog whimpered and hurried off in the other direction. The man was then paralyzed with fear when he saw a ghostly male figure pass between the trees and disappear. In 2006, a camera crew from Hipposcope Films visited the site to make a documentary called *Cane Hill: From the Inside*. They, too, saw the ghostly male figure, although in one of the hallways of the building this time. In 2010, the hospital was consumed by a fire of unknown origin.

The hauntings continued for a time before the building was demolished to make way for housing units. There have been no reports of hauntings at the new homes. It seems the unhappy spirits of the Cane Hill Lunatic Asylum have finally been laid to rest.

Online Resources

Other mysterious titles by Charles River Editors

Other folk history titles by Charles River Editors

Other titles about England on Amazon

Further Reading

Ackroyd, Peter. *London: The Biography.* London: Vintage, 2001.

Adams, Paul and Peter Underwood. *Shadows in the Nave: A Guide to the Haunted Churches of England.* Stroud, Gloucestershire, United Kingdom: The History Press, 2011.

Chambers, Paul. Cock Lane Ghost: *Murder, Sex and Haunting in Dr. Johnson's London.* Stroud, Gloucestershire, United Kingdom: The History Press, 2006.

Charles River Editors and Sean McLachlan. *Mysterious England: Monsters, Mysteries, and Magic Across the English Nation.* Charles River Editors, 2016.

Charles River Editors and Sean McLachlan. *Mysterious London: A History of Ancient Mysteries, Odd Individuals, and Unusual Legends across the English Capital.* Charles River Editors, 2016.

Glinert, Ed. *The London Compendium: A Street-by-Street Exploration of the Hidden Metropolis.* London: Penguin, 2003.

Green, Andrew. *Our Haunted Kingdom: more than 350 authenticated hauntings or case histories recorded in the UK over the past 25 years.* London, United Kingdom: Wolfe Publishing Ltd, 1973.

Harper, Charles G. *Tales of the Supernatural: With Some Account of Hereditary Curses and Family Legends.* London: Chapman & Hall, Ltd., 1907.

Ingram, John. *The Haunted Homes and Family Traditions of Great Britain.* London: Gibbings & Company, Ltd., 1897.

Jones, Richard. *Walking Haunted London: 25 Original Walks Exploring London's Ghostly Past.* Northampton, MA: Interlink Pub Group Inc, 2007.

Maple, Eric. *Supernatural England.* London: Robert Hale Ltd, 1977.

Marsden, Simon. *This Spectred Isle: A Journey through Haunted England.* New York City: Barnes & Noble, 2006.

Matthews, John and Chesca Potter, eds. *The Aquarian Guide to Legendary London.* Wellingborough, Northamptonshire: The Aquarian Press, 1990.

McLachlan, Sean. *Moon Handbooks London.* Emeryville, California: Avalon Travel Publishing, 2007.

Rennison, Nick. *The London Blue Plaque Guide.* Thrupp, Stroud, Gloucestershire: Sutton Publishing, 2003.

Underwood, Peter. *Haunted London.* London: Amberly Publishing, 2010.

Westwood, Jennifer and Jacqueline Simpson. *The Lore of the Land: A Guide to England's Legends, from Spring-Heeled Jack to the Witches of Warboys.* London: Penguin Publishing Company, 2005.

Wilson, Colin. *Poltergeist: A Classic Study in Destructive Hauntings.* Woodbury, MN: Llewellyn Publications, 2009.

Free Books by Charles River Editors

We have brand new titles available for free most days of the week. To see which of our titles are currently free, click on this link.

Discounted Books by Charles River Editors

We have titles at a discount price of just 99 cents everyday. To see which of our titles are currently 99 cents, click on this link.

Printed in Great Britain
by Amazon